Mandala Coloring Book V.2

Meditation Alternative

Andrea T. Cross

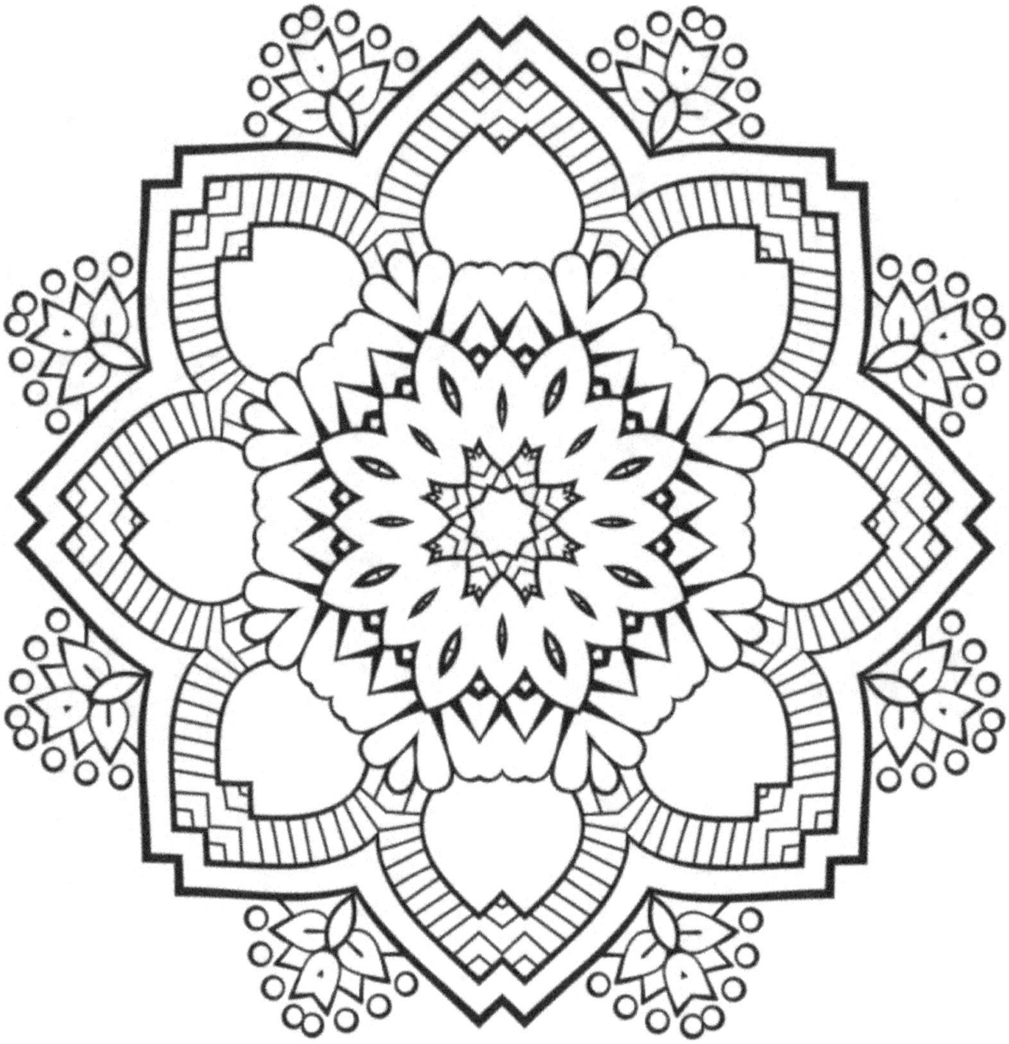

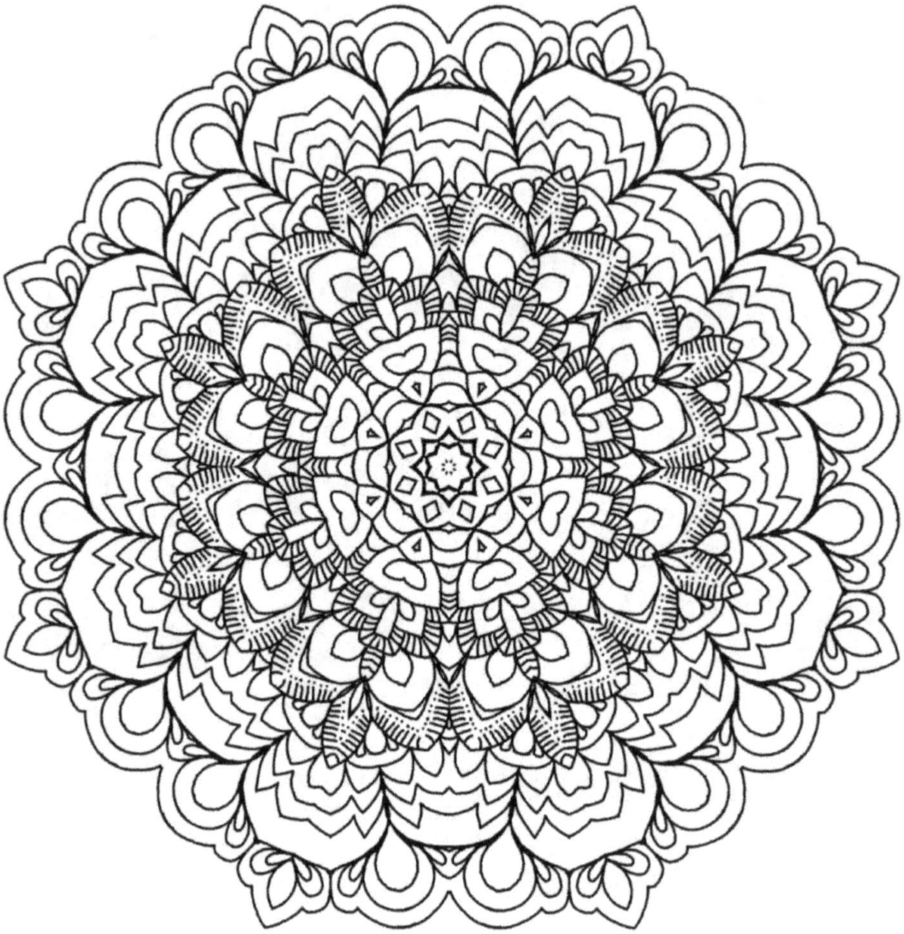

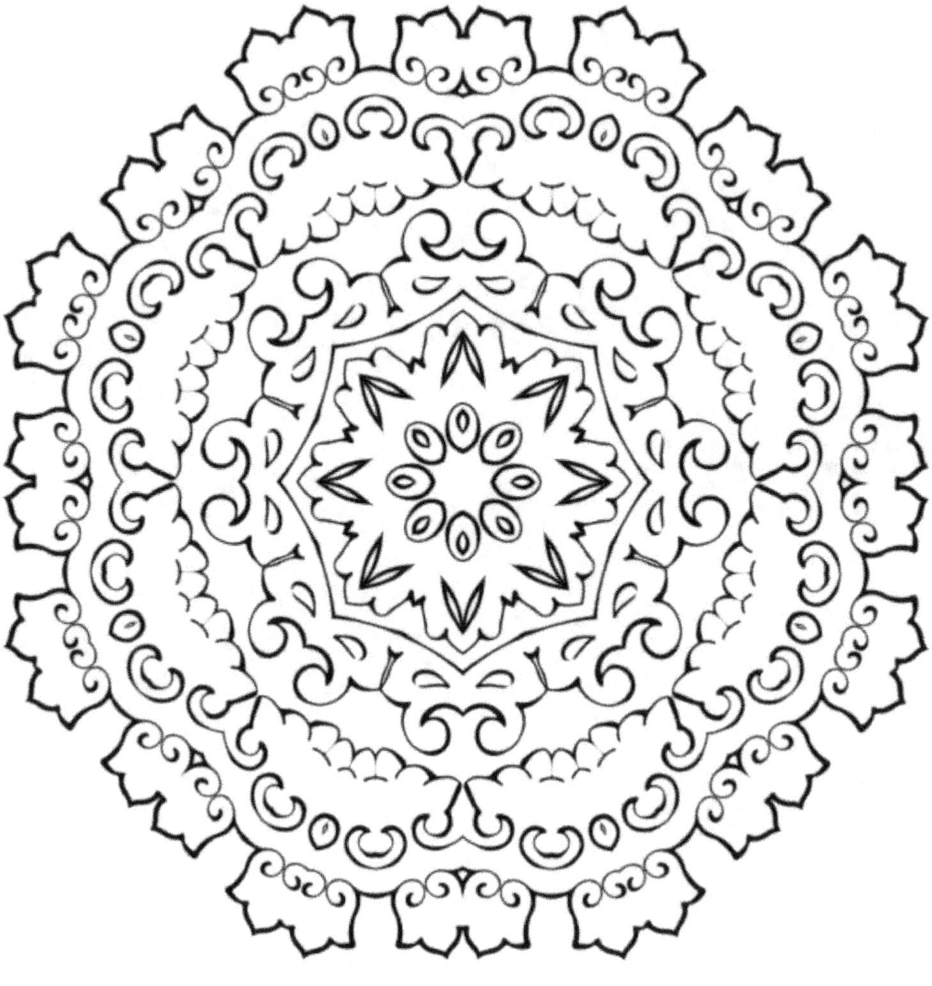

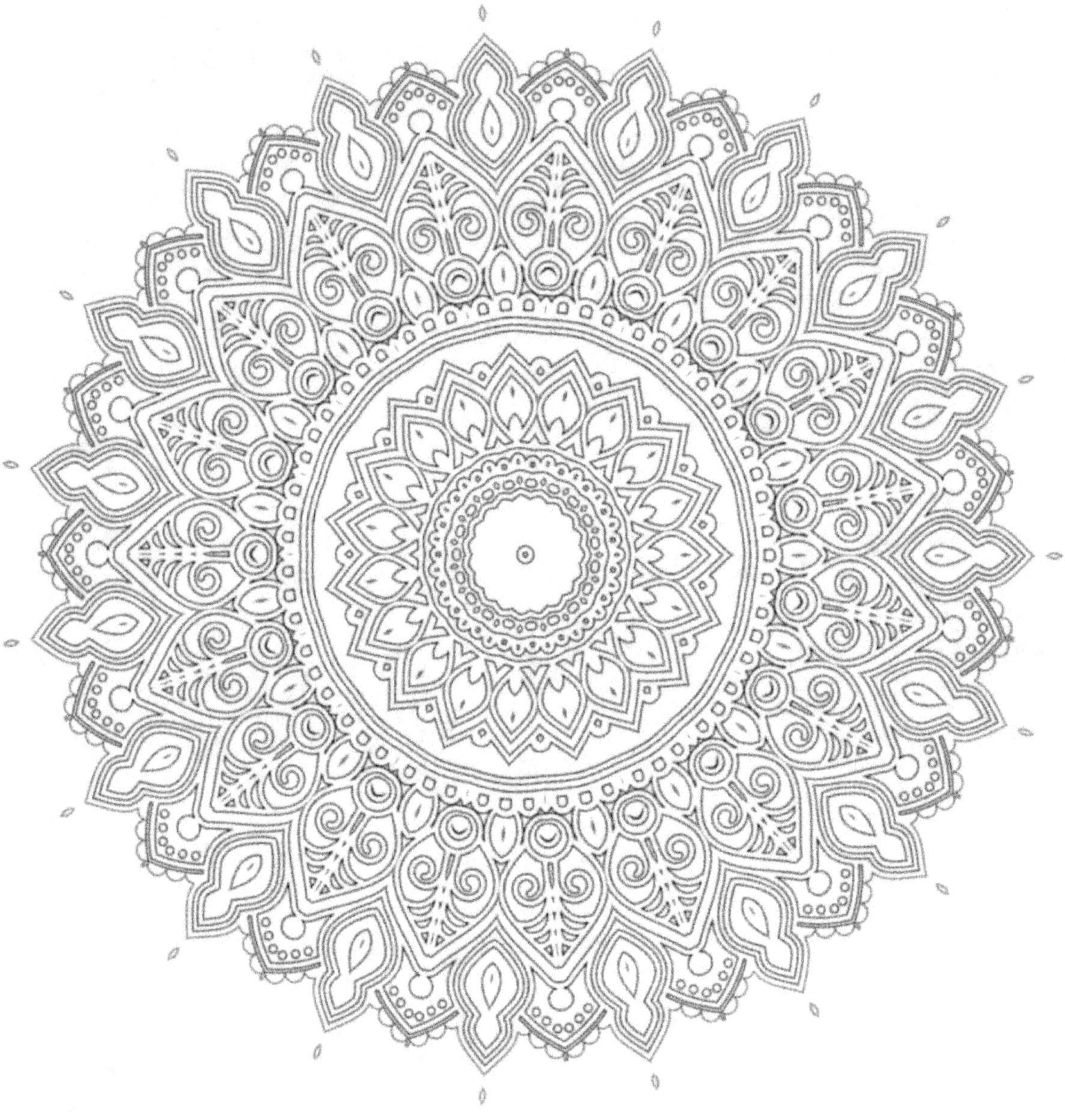

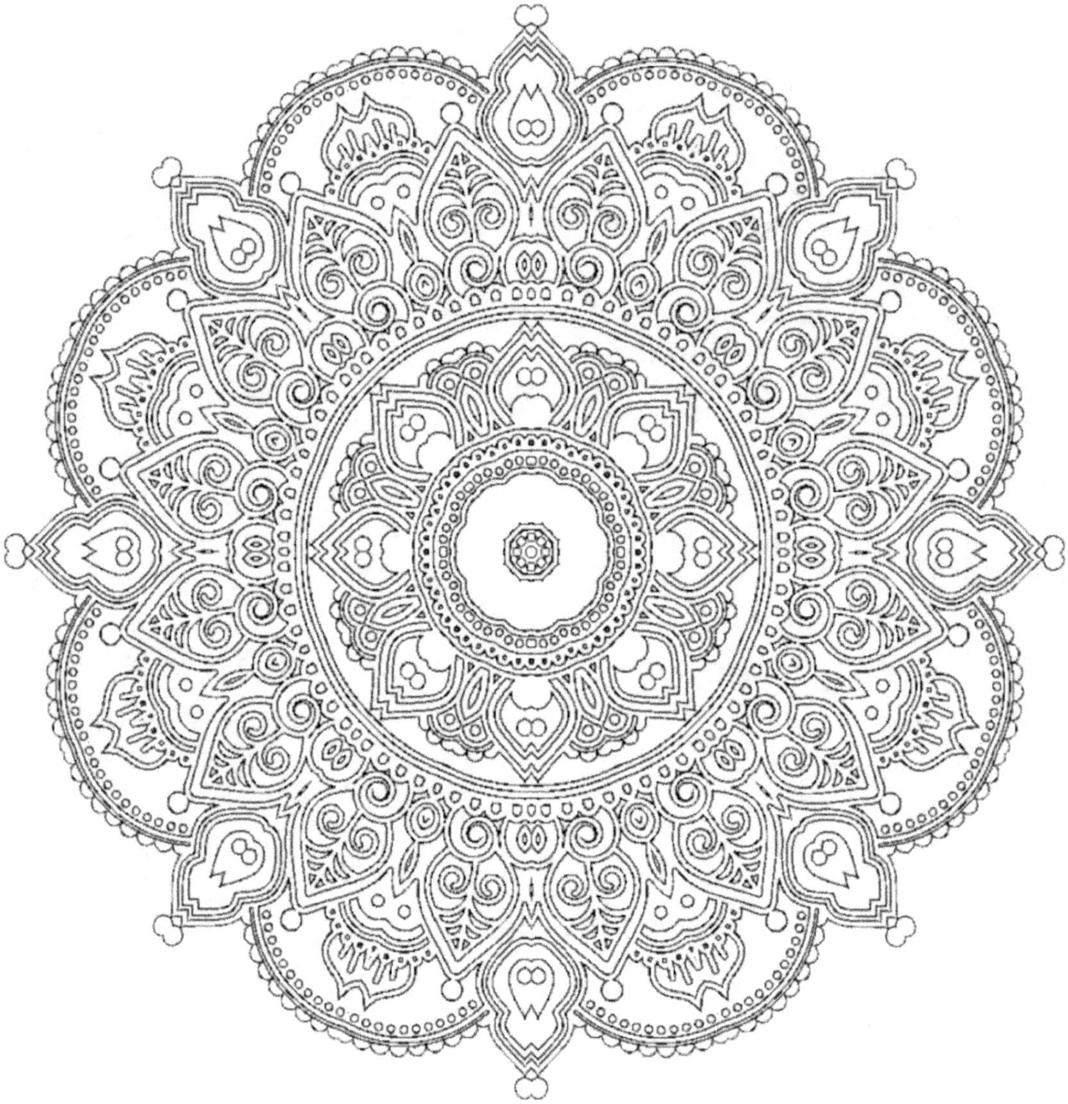

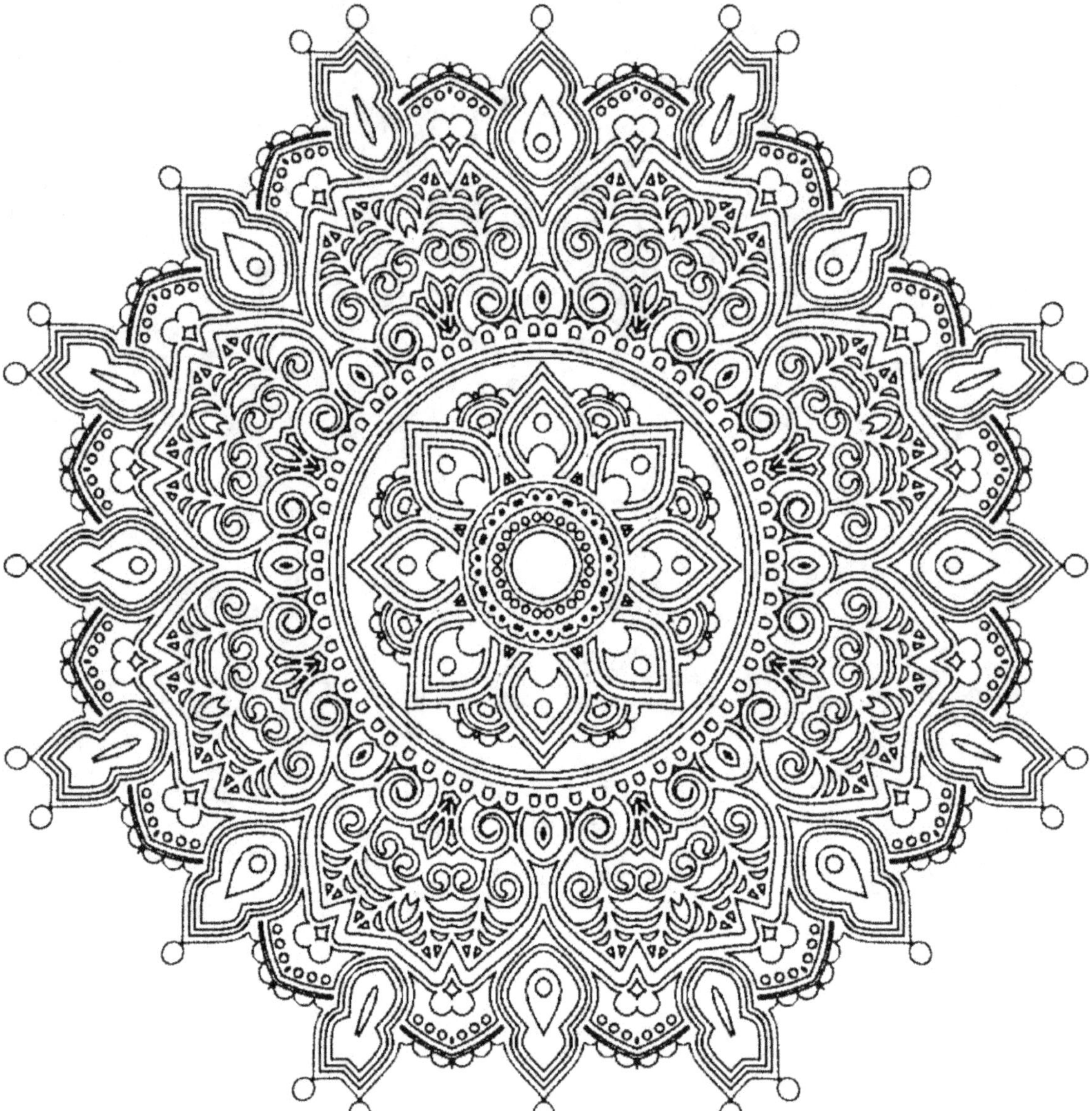

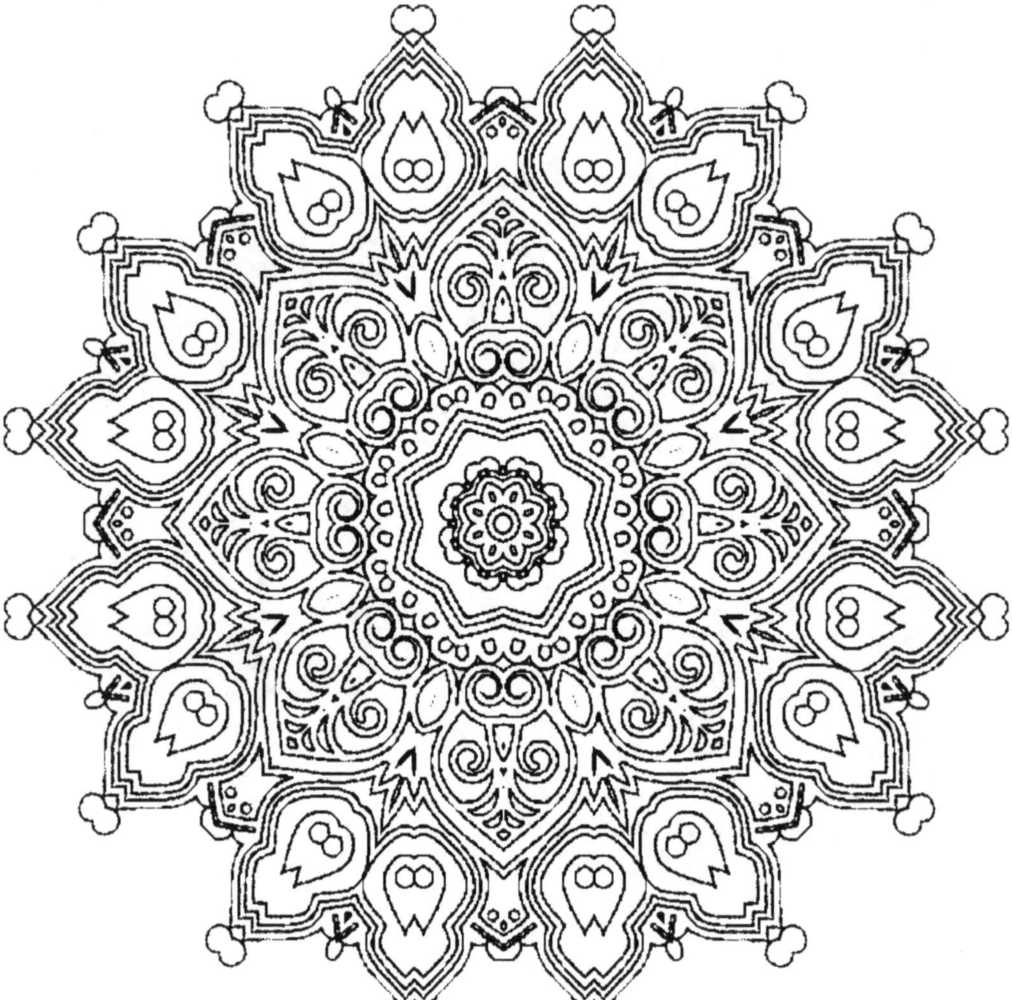

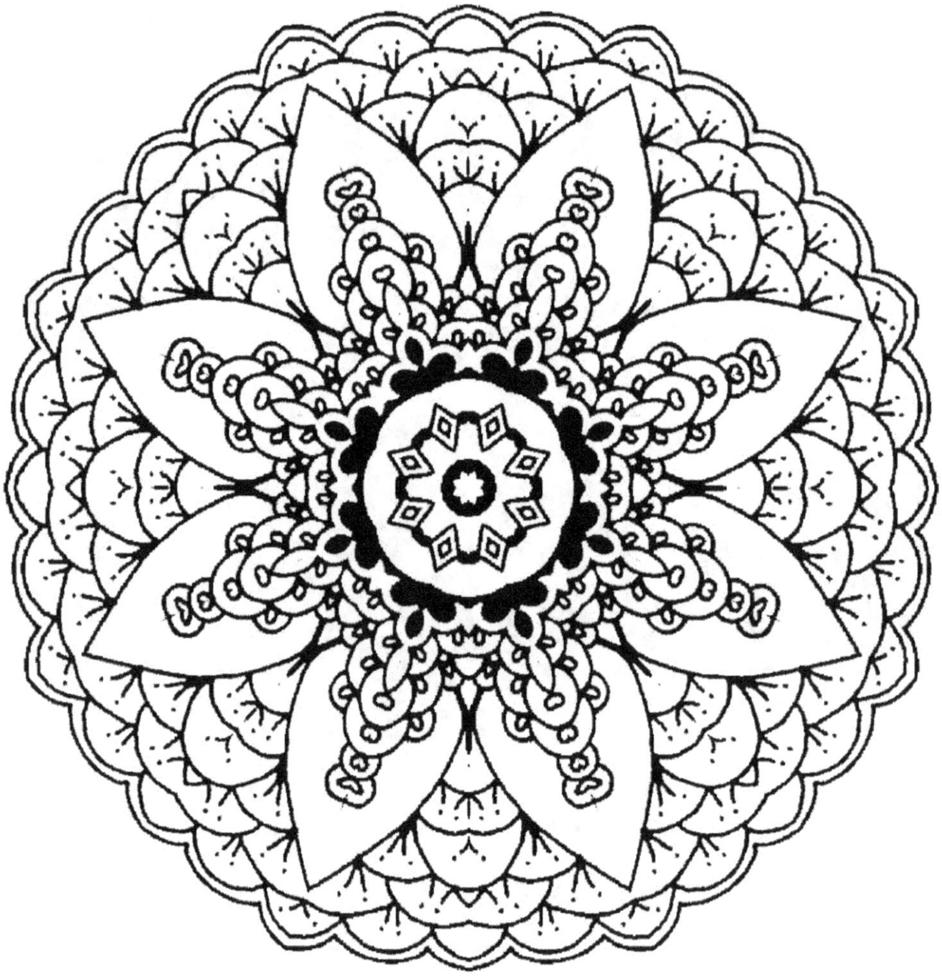

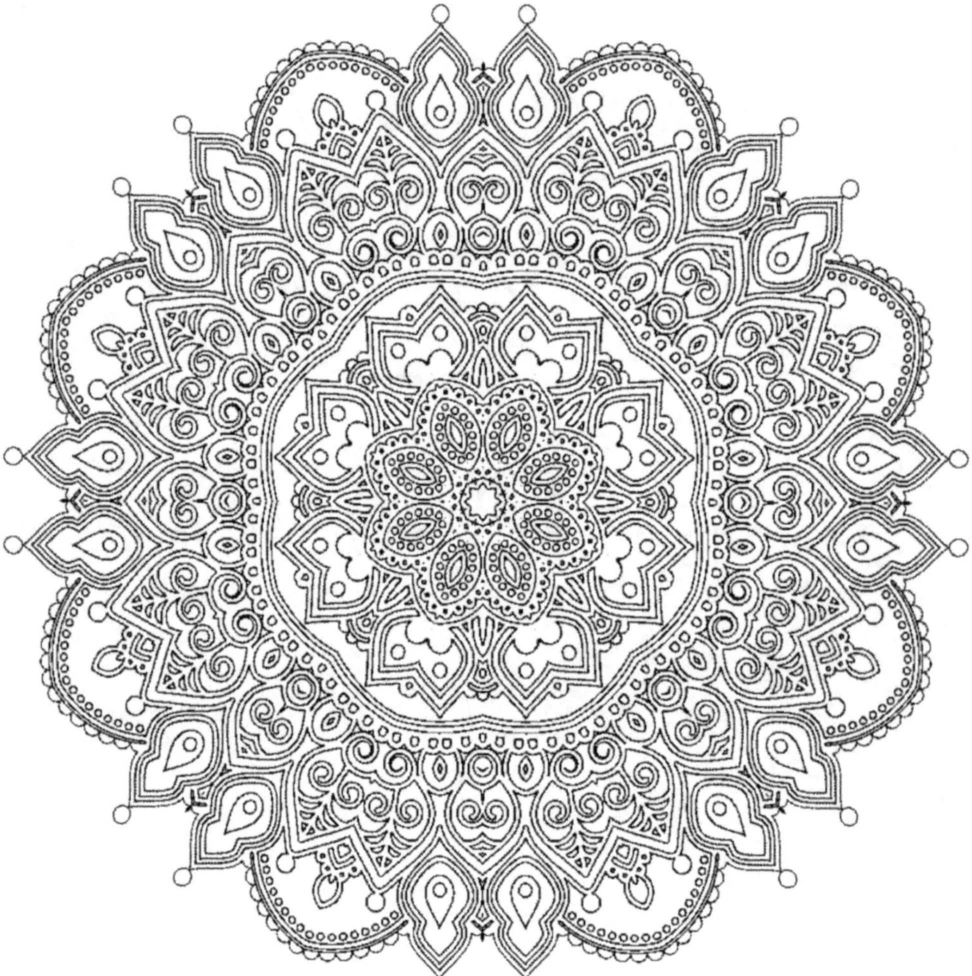

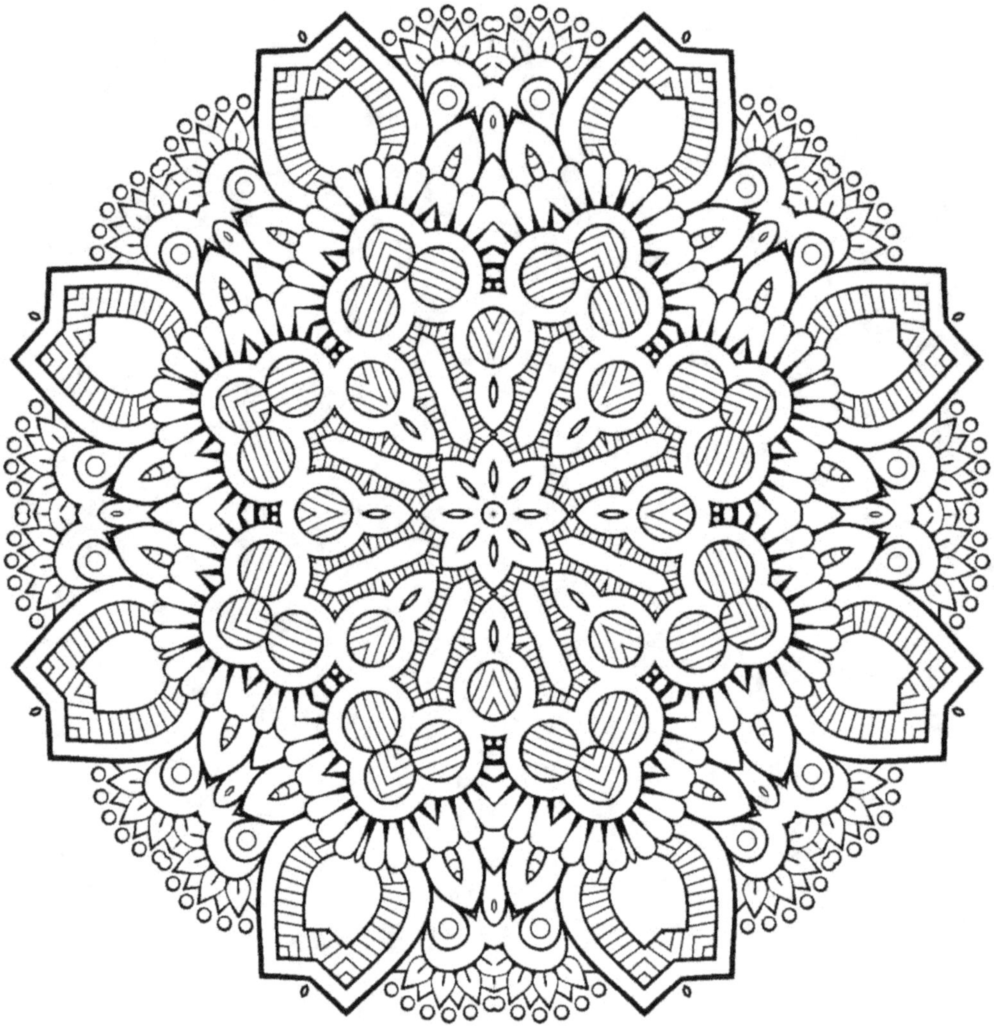

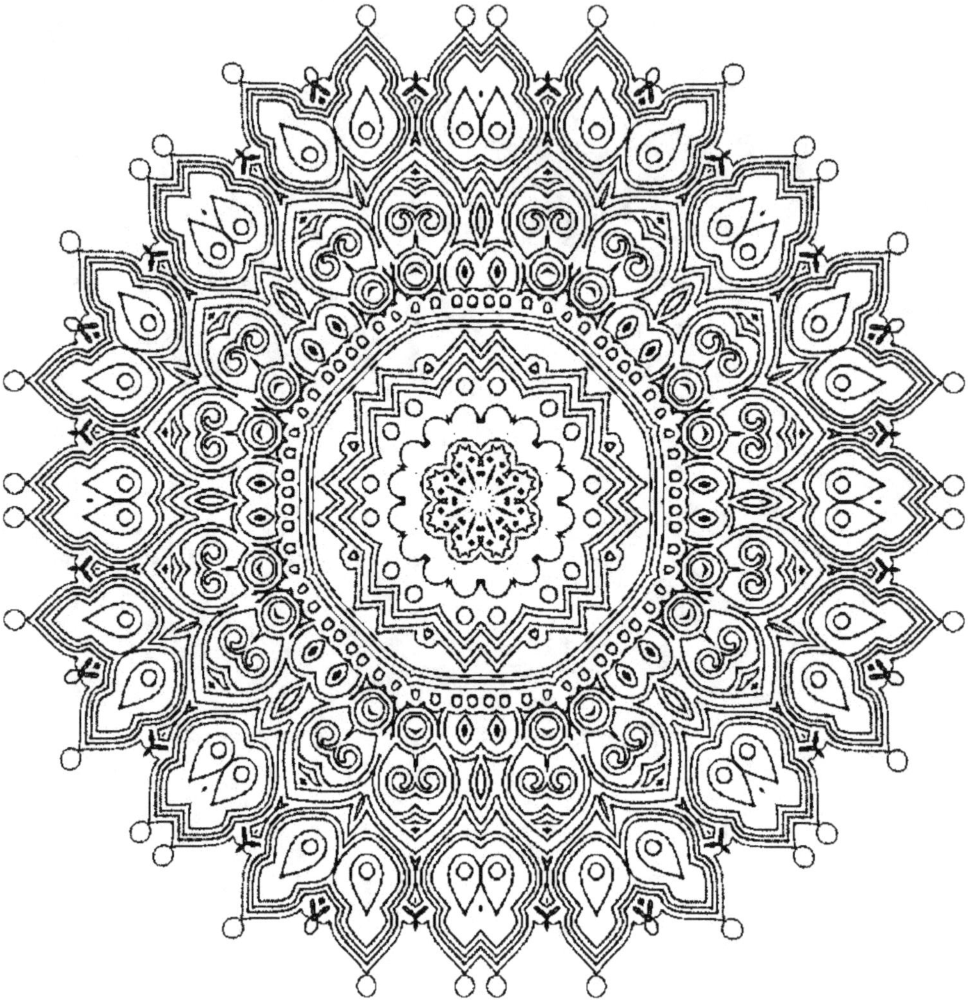

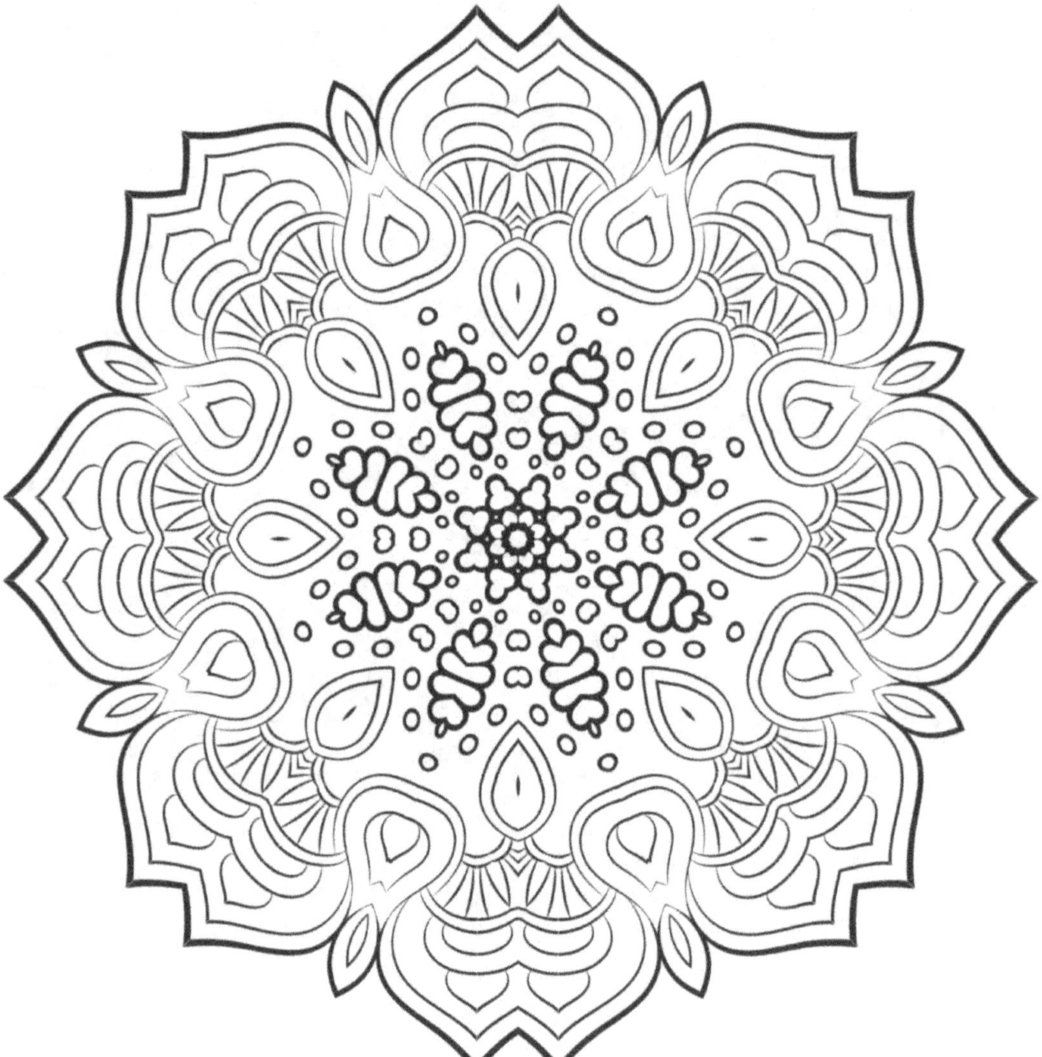

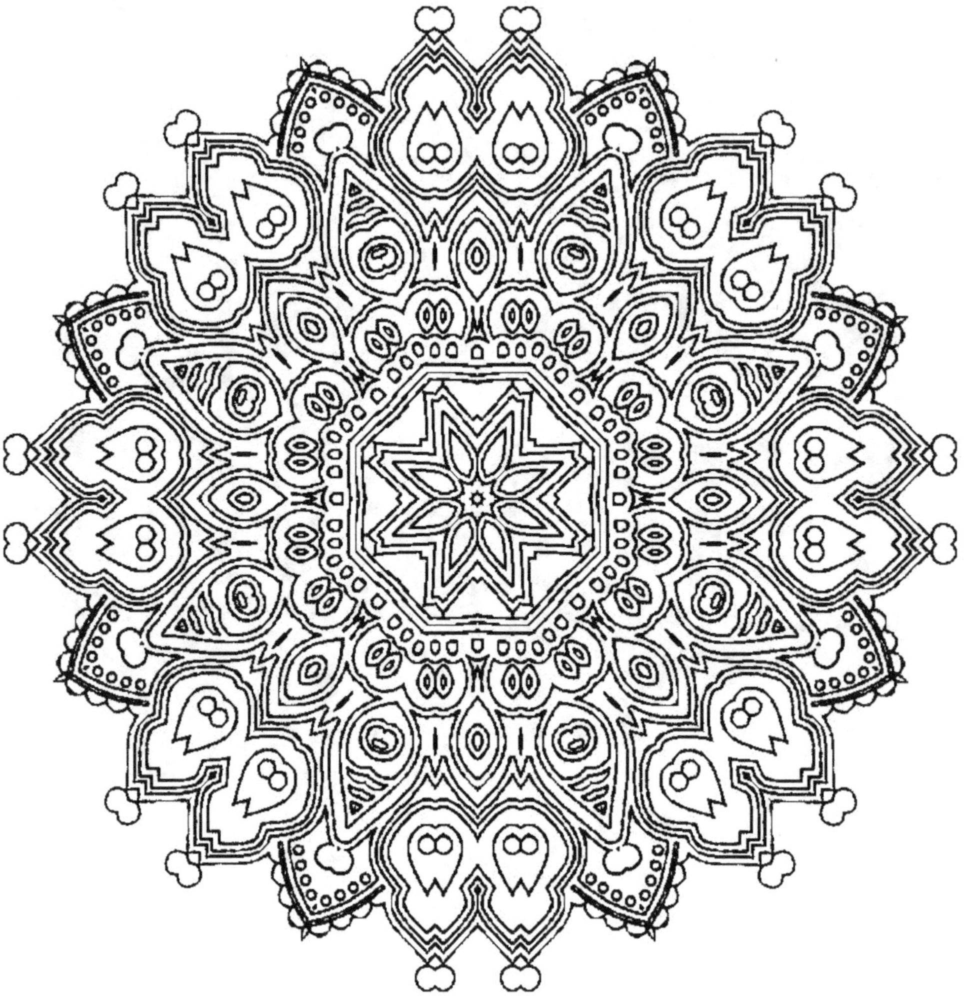

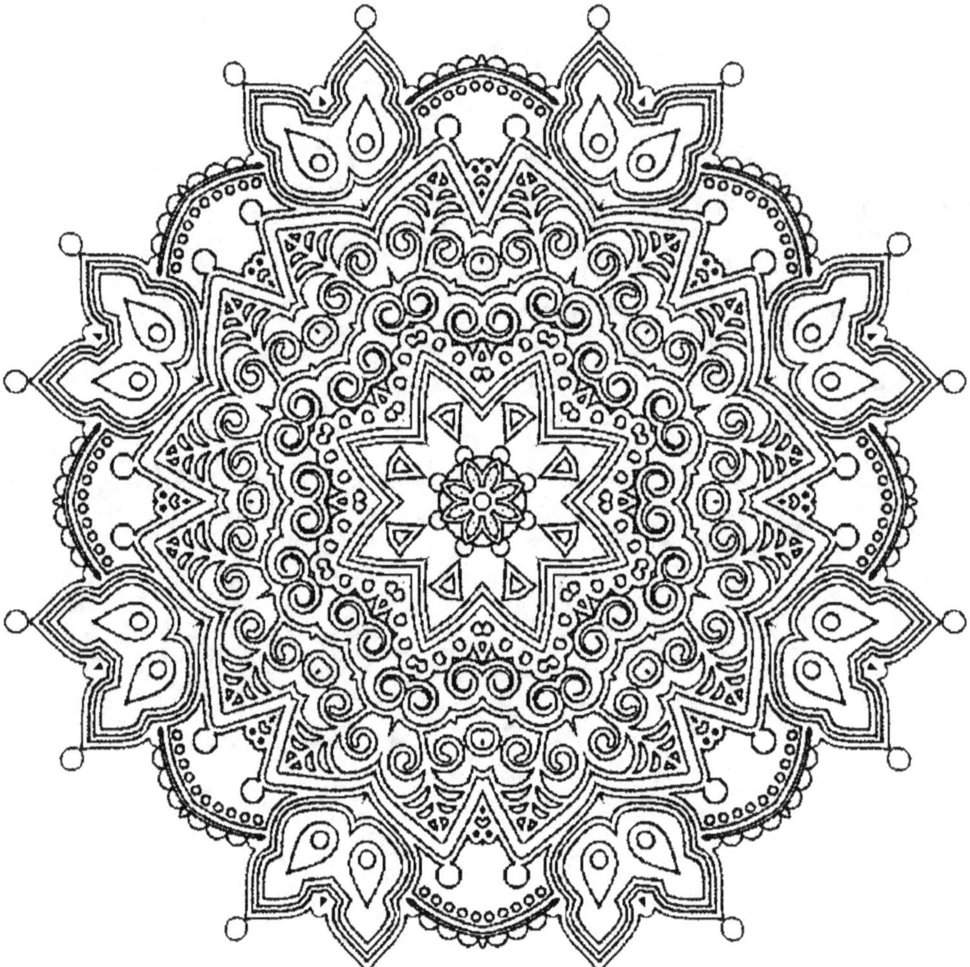

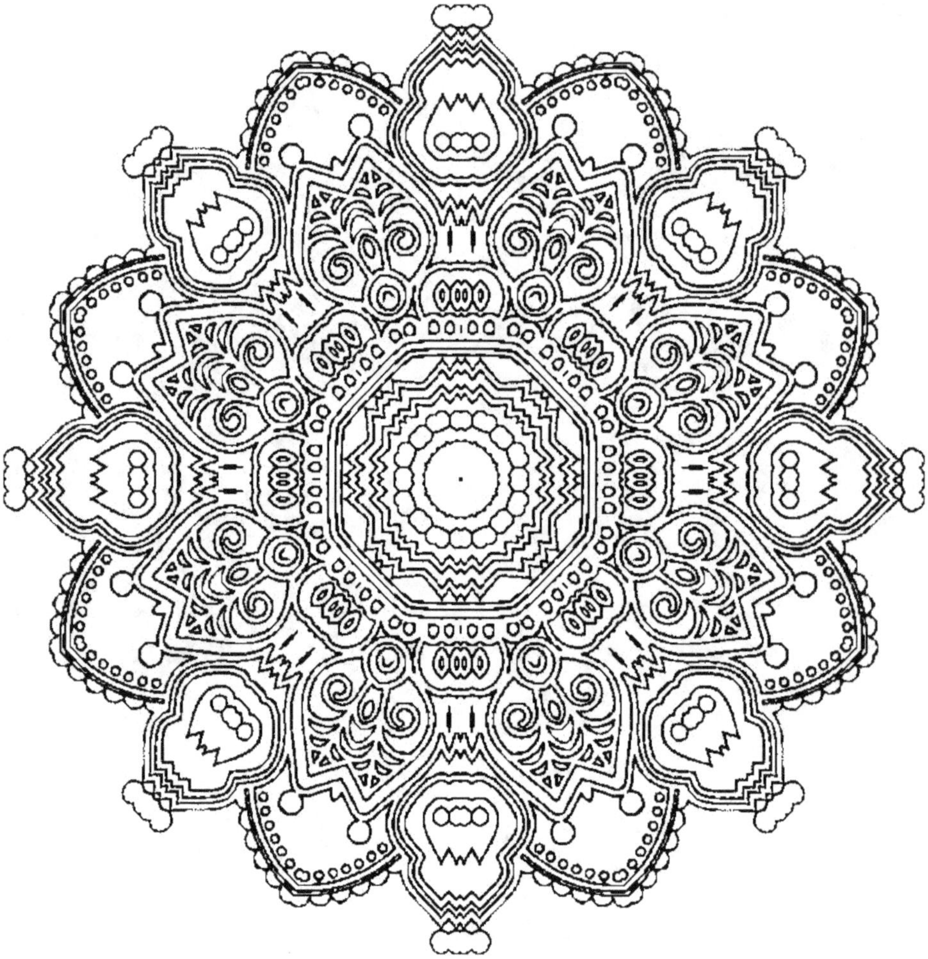

www.ingramcontent.com/pod-product-compliance
Lightning Source LLC
Chambersburg PA
CBHW080629220526
45467CB00011B/3428
* 9 7 8 1 7 0 3 6 1 3 6 5 0 *